Spilling the Beans on...

MAKING IT IN THE

MOVIES

First published in 2001 by Miles Kelly Publishing,
Bardfield Centre, Great Bardfield, Essex CM7 4SL

Printed in Italy

ISBN 1-84236-013-2

2468109753I

Cover design and illustration: Inc
Layout design: Mackerel

Spilling the Beans on...

MAKING IT IN THE

MOVIES

by **Martin Oliver**

Illustrations   Martin Remphry

Miles Kelly
PUBLISHING

Titles in the Series:

Making it in Football

Making it in Music

Making it in the Movies

Making it in the Ballet

Making it in the Fashion Industry

Making it in Computers

Contents

About the Author

Martin Oliver has written over 20 fiction and non-fiction books for children. His interest in the movies started at the early age of five when he saw *Bambi*, although he did cry. Currently his favourite film is *Toy Story 2*. He lives in southwest London with his wife, and his two children who he loves taking to the local kids' cinema club.

Opening scene

he date: 1895. *The location*: the small basement of a café in Paris. *The scene*: 35 people are slowly sitting down, chatting noisily as they wait for the unveiling of the Cinématographe, the latest invention from Auguste and Louis Lumière.

Suddenly the lights are dimmed. There is a humming noise like a sewing machine and a beam of light projects across the small room on to the opposite wall. As the first few shaky images appear, there is complete silence. After a few moments, gasps of amazement are heard followed by shouts of astonishment – then applause. The audience

cheer and clap as the lights
go on after about ten
minutes. They have just
seen the world's first
moving pictures and
witnessed the birth of the
movie industry.

After that first showing,
word quickly spread about
the miracle of moving pictures. Within weeks,
thousands of people were queuing around the
corner to see the Lumière's movie show. As the
popularity of films extended around the world,
they caused riots – one movie of a train arriving at
a station made the terrified audience run away
when they thought the express would burst through
the wall – and they've been going at full steam
ever since.

From that first showing in Paris, the movie
industry exploded into one of the biggest and most
exciting in the world. It transformed the sleepy
Californian town of Hollywood into one of the most

famous places on the planet and created a whole new series of happy – and sometimes unhappy – endings for people working within it.

Over the next few pages, you'll get the low-down on life in the film business. We uncover the good, the bad and sometimes the ugly side of movies. We spill the beans on some of the larger-than-life characters who have appeared on the big screen and we even include snapshots of the good – and not so good – points of being a movie star.

So, if you think you're ready to be put in the picture, just grab some popcorn, make yourself comfortable and settle down in a front row seat as we begin…

Spilling the Beans on …

the Movie Industry

Wishing on a star

Who knows where it all began? Perhaps on the sofa watching your favourite video, acting in the school play or even during a visit to your local cinema? Suddenly, an idea comes into your head: 'Why can't it be me? Why can't I be biffing the bad guys, looking fantastic or performing the most hair-raising stunts around?'

It's hardly surprising that most people wish that they could be in the movie industry. Almost everyone, including kings and queens, are major movie fans. Even Queen Victoria, who was famous for not being amused by almost everything, loved films – and it's true that on the silver screen everything seems bigger, better and more exciting than everyday life.

The more you think about being in films, the better it gets. Along with presidents, pop stars and supermodels, movie idols are the most famous people in the world. You get to visit amazing places, hobnob with other amazing people – oh yes, and there's usually a few zillion dollars thrown in on the side. You've seen some performances on screen and thought that you could do better (well, even a tree could do better than some), so why not you?

You probably won't be surprised to hear that you're not the first person to have this idea but you might be surprised to hear how stars were treated in the early days of the movie industry.

FANTASTIC FILM FACT

On early film sets, actors were considered far less important than the camera or other valuable things such as props or even horses.

For over fifteen years, the names of actors didn't even appear on the credits because films were considered far inferior to the theatre. As a result, many movie actors wanted to keep quiet about appearing on screen as it was seen as a sign of failure.

However, things changed in 1910 when Florence Laurence became the first true movie star. What do you think helped her rise to stardom?

a she married a prince

b she featured in a fake newspaper story

c she was the first actress to talk on screen

Answer:

b. Publicity stunts are part and parcel of the movie industry. Florence Laurence had become popular after appearing in a series of black and white films although her name had not appeared on the credits. Producer, Carl Laemmle, poached her from a rival studio then made up a fake news story about her being tragically killed in a car crash. Once her profile had been raised, he placed an ad saying that she was actually alive and was about to star in a new movie.

Despite such bad beginnings, the rise to stardom of Florence Laurence soon convinced reluctant early actors that being a star was no bad thing after all. Superstar status was soon followed by superstar salaries and superstar lifestyles. As these attractions have got bigger each year so have the numbers of people thinking about becoming a star.

So, how do you turn your dreams into reality? Once you've decided on pursuing an Oscar-winning career in the motion picture business, we can help you get off on the right track to movie success with your first major decision – what sort of star do you want to be?

Leading man or leading lady

Let's face it, when did you last see a movie star who looks like the back end of a bus? To play the leading role in a smash hit movie, you'll need to look not just good, but amazing. Take a long hard look at yourself in the mirror (if you don't, plenty of others will) and ask yourself if you really were born to play James Bond or Mary Poppins.

Pimples, wrinkles or even an ounce of spare flesh are all serious no-no's. Of course, if you've got the looks and are willing to spend hours toning, tanning and turning your nose up at your favourite food, you may be in with a chance.

On the positive side, once you've made it as a star, you'll enjoy the adoration of millions of fans and you can charge up to $30 million per movie. On the downside, you'll enjoy the adoration of millions of fans but you'll also need to keep your looks for as long as you can. It may be unfair but as a leading man, you'll probably have an advantage. You're allowed to get older (although you'll probably need a wig) and you'll usually earn more than your leading ladies.

There is one way of cheating – by visiting your friendly, local plastic surgeon. It's not pleasant and

it's often painful but there are plenty of stars who've secretly popped in for a nip and tuck – and sometimes even more. Look out for tell-tale signs of gravity-defying skin and a large dent in your bank balance.

Character actor

If you're not physically perfect enough to be a leading man or lady, then join the other 99.9% of the human race. Character actors play all those other roles besides the main characters and while it is very rare, some character actors do manage to become stars in their own right. Danny DeVito breaks all the golden rules of being a leading man. He's bald, a bit chubby and less than 1.63 metres tall, yet he's still managed to become a big star in films like *Matilda* and *Twins*.

The good news for character actors is that you'll probably be given a wider range of roles, may well be busier and enjoy a longer film career.

The bad news is that you'll probably have to keep acting as you won't get such huge pots of money. If it's fame you're after, you'll have to get used to people looking at you and whispering, "Isn't that, you-know-who? They were in what's-its-name on the telly."

Child star

If you're in rush to be a star, you may want to start right away. Movie-makers are always looking for new talent and throughout the history of the film industry, child actors have often been the biggest little movie stars around.

Sounds great, doesn't it? Instead of hopping onto the school bus taking you to a geography exam, you could be hopping into a chauffeur-driven limousine taking you to the set of your latest blockbuster. If you're lucky, you could be like Anna Paquin who won an Oscar when she was nine years old for *The Piano*, you could be like Drew Barrymore who starred in *ET: the Extra Terrestrial* at the age of seven, like Jonathan Lipnicki who was eight when he appeared in *Stuart Little* or even like Macaulay Culkin.

Macaulay *who?*

Exactly! Macaulay Culkin was one of the biggest stars of the 1990s. He appeared in the *Home Alone* films, pocketing up to $8 million a time. So what happened to him?

Macaulay made the worst possible career move – he grew up! While child stars are in demand as cute kids, their faces often don't fit when they get older. The result? After a certain time there's no such thing as a happy birthday because getting older often marks 'The End' of their movie career.

After years in the spotlight, becoming famous and making friends with adult stars, many child actors find it hard to get used to a more 'normal' life. In the last few years, Macaulay's got married and separated, lost touch completely with his father and he's now trying to stage his first comeback – all this and he's still only in his 20s.

Star quality

Now you know exactly what sort of star you want to be, you're ready to launch yourself on that glittering career. However, before you set out, it's worth considering for that $6 million question – what do you need to be a star?

If anyone told you that they knew the answer to that question, they'd be lying. The truth is that no one can put their finger on the key to movie success. Luckily, you can save yourself lots of time and energy – not to mention heartache – by checking out if you've got the star qualities listed below. You may not need all of them but the more you have, the better your chances.

1. Pushy Parents

Behind every child star, you'll usually find at least one pushy parent. Generally a frustrated actor themselves, they'll do all they can to get their children into the spotlight. Find out more with our good, bad and ugly guide.

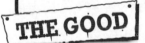

THE GOOD

Pushy parents will do just about anything to get you on the stage. They'll sacrifice their own career, drive you about from audition to audition, pay for all those singing, dancing and acting lessons and make sure you're happy when you're on set. What's more, it can work! Judy Garland was put on the stage at the age of

six and she went on to play the leading
role in *The Wizard of Oz*.

 **THE BAD.**

If you do have a pushy parent, it might be
a good idea to keep an eye on where the
money's going. Jackie Coogan was a huge
star who first appeared on screen when he
was 18 months old and went on to appear
in many of Charlie Chaplin's films in the
1910s and 20s. Over the next few years, he
was rumoured to have earned $4 million
but unfortunately while he was out
earning, his mum was out spending and he
ended up with less than $125,000.

THE UGLY

One pushy parent went too far in 1938
when two children aged eight and ten were
found outside the central casting office in
Los Angeles. The children explained that

their mum had put them on the bus and sent them thousands of miles from Detroit to Hollywood. She had instructed them to send for the rest of the family once they'd made a fortune in the movies. Eventually, the unlucky duo were sent home again.

2. Thick Skin

You'll need to put up with plenty of rejections and put-downs before your true star qualities are recognised. When 50s movie star, Rock Hudson, was starting out as a young actor, his first screen test was actually used as a demonstration to other star-struck hopefuls on how not to act. Clark Gable who went on to be a huge Hollywood star was described as a big ape by one studio boss while Dustin Hoffman who played Peter Pan's mortal enemy in the film *Hook*, and whose movie career spans nearly forty years, was voted by fellow members of his acting school class as 'least likely to succeed'.

3. Never say 'no'

Always take any opportunity to appear on screen – whatever it is. Many movie idols like Clint Eastwood, Marilyn Monroe and Clark Gable all started off as lowly extras before they were spotted and found themselves in the spotlight. Meanwhile, Anthony Quinn's Oscar-winning career began when he pretended not just that he could speak Cheyenne but also that he could ride a horse. By the time the producers realised he couldn't do either, he was already cast in the film and it was too late to replace him.

4. Be tough

Being a star always looks so effortless, doesn't it? Unfortunately, it takes a whole lot of hard work to make things look that simple.

Are you tough enough to hack it? Find out in our killer questionnaire.

1 You're appearing in the movie *Titanic*. Your costume is heavy and you feel as if you are coming down with pneumonia. Then the director announces that he's shooting the flood scene where you are swamped by thousands of tonnes of icy water. Do you...

 a Demand that the water is heated up before you'll be in the scene?

 b Tell the director that you aren't feeling well and cancel the shoot?

 c Agree to the shooting schedule?

2 You're delighted to be given the leading role in a film called *The Elephant Man* but less than delighted when you go into make-up. Is this because...

a The make-up makes you look ugly?

b The bright lights give you a headache?

c It takes seven hours to apply and you can't eat at all once it's on?

3 You're appearing in a thriller and are about to be filmed being attacked by birds. On the day of shooting, the director surprises you with some news. Is it...

a He's agreed with your demands to get a stand-in for you?

b He understands that you don't like birds and will use special effects instead?

c He will be using real birds to attack you, lured by food attached to your clothes?

4 You've landed one of the leading roles in a Hollywood musical opposite a screen legend. You've been practising one routine for hours and your feet are killing you. Do you...

a Throw a tantrum. You know all the moves – it's time to go home?

b Complain and take the next week off?

c Continue to practise until you're perfect – and your feet are bleeding?

So, how did you do?

Mostly a's

Good try. You're obviously brave enough to stand up for yourself but you're unlikely to get these kinds of special favours on set.

Mostly b's

Oh dear. What a wimp – you're really not tough enough to stand up to being a star.

Mostly c's

Congratulations, you're tough enough. All these things actually happened to movie stars. Kate Winslett was almost drowned during the making of *Titanic* and John Hurt had to battle with his horrible make-up in *The Elephant Man.* Tippi Hedren almost had her eye pecked out by a seagull in *The Birds* while many unfortunate co-stars soon discovered how hard Fred Astaire drove himself to make his dance steps look effortless.

5. Be happy to change yourself

What's in a name? Well, quite a lot it would seem. Plenty of stars have changed their names – and a lot more besides – in order to get their big break. If you're a

British actor, you have to choose a stage name when you become a member of Equity, the trading union for actors. Most try their original name but sometimes it's already been taken. The easiest solution is to add an initial. As a result, you may have heard of Richard E. Grant but probably not of the lesser-known, plain old Richard Grant.

However, some stars go for a much bigger name change – and it's not hard to see why. Can you match the original name to the star?

1 Tom Cruise

2 John Wayne

3 Michael Caine

4 Stan Laurel

A Arthur S Jefferson

B Thomas Mapother IV

C Marion Morrison

MARION MORRISON

D Maurice Micklewhite Jnr

Answers: 1B, 2C, 3D, 4A.

A new name is just the beginning for some star-struck hopefuls. Margarita Cansino was a Spanish dancer in the 30s who probably went a little further than most people. What did you think she decided to change in order to get her big screen break?

1 Her name

2 Her accent

3 Her nationality

4 Her appearance

Answer: all of them.

Margarita decided that she needed a complete movie makeover to succeed. As a result, she went to voice training to change her accent, she had all the hairs removed by electrolysis from her hairline and dyed her black hair red. She then changed her name and re-invented herself as an American actress – Rita Hayworth. Luckily for Rita, it all worked and she became a major star for over three decades.

6. Get lucky

Perhaps luck is the most important star quality of all. One leading lady got her big break after being seen in her father's car by a passing director while Natalie Portman (who stars in the latest Stars Wars films) was plucked from obscurity when she was spotted sitting in a pizza parlour. The star qualities of Harrison Ford (who appeared as Han Solo in the original Stars Wars movies) were only recognised when he happened to be working as a carpenter in the film studios where they were casting for the film.

Acting ability?

Congratulations and a fake Oscar if you spotted the one star quality that's been missed out – brilliant acting skill.

It might seem like a strange question but how important is it? Character actors need to be versatile but how often do leading men and women actually act? Take a big star like Arnold Schwarzenegger or Julia Roberts and ask yourself how many times you're getting immersed into their character rather than just watching them on screen.

Of course, this doesn't mean that you should ignore your acting classes although some stars make it all sound very easy.

The Michael Caine Masterclass

When asked what was his secret for screen acting success, Michael Caine simply replied, "don't blink".

Acting the part

When it comes to acting, there are two schools of thought. With the more traditional European approach, actors do the necessary research then turn up on set and act their part as their character. Once the camera stops, they go back to being themselves.

However, with method acting, there is a completely different approach. Method actors are encouraged to immerse themselves and experience life through their characters. As a result, method actors often insist on staying in character even when they aren't being filmed.

Sounds like a good idea, doesn't it? Well, it might be if your character is charming, witty and generous with presents, but what if you're meant to be playing a loud, objectionable murderer with bad breath?

Some stars go even further to make sure they're really living their role. Check out our Method

Madness Film Fact section.

1 Before filming the
   Vietnam war movie,
   Platoon, the cast spent
   two weeks training in
   the Philippines with a
   former marine to ensure
   they looked like real
   soldiers.

2 To prepare for his role
   as an injured soldier in
   Birdy, Nicolas Cage
   spent five weeks with
   his head wrapped in
   bandages and had two
   teeth taken out without
   pain relief. He went one
   step further in the
   horror film, *Vampire
   Kiss,* when he
   volunteered to eat a live
   cockroach.

3 Why bother acting an overweight prize fighter? Robert de Niro saved pounds on the make-up and special effects budget by piling on the pounds with a diet of hamburgers and pizza in order to play the character of real-life boxing champion, Jake LaMotta, in *Raging Bull*.

Reach for the stars

Now you've got an idea of the star qualities required, are you still feeling up to the task?

Good, thought so. In an ideal world, you'll be tougher than Sly Stallone, more adaptable than a chameleon and have enough charisma to re-launch the Titanic. When it comes to acting, singing or dancing, you make the Hollywood greats look like absolute beginners – well, in the privacy of your bedroom at least. So, now comes the big step. How do you go from an audience of five family members to an audience of five million worldwide? How do you transform yourself from high school heart throb to Hollywood heart throb?

Before we point you in the right direction it's time for another piece of advice: *don't give up the day job.*

Even with every single star quality under your belt, it's best to be prepared for a long haul. Everyone's heard stories of instant stardom but the truth is that most overnight successes have actually got years of hard work and experience under their belts. You'll need to be prepared for a hard slog to reach the top of the bill and you'll have to keep yourself fed, clothed and housed while you're waiting for that elusive big break.

Some famous names who've reached the top had to come from a long way down. It's a movie industry joke that every waiter in Los Angeles has got a theatre school degree and a script in their back pocket while a glance at the CV of even the biggest stars will reveal a host of jobs from coffin-maker to checkout assistant.

However, there are a few short cuts that make your route to the top a lot quicker. Check them out to see if you're already ahead of the competition.

1. Be famous already

There are plenty of stars who had already made a big name for themselves before stepping out in front of the cameras. Arnold Schwarzenegger launched his acting career on the back of winning the Mr Universe bodybuilding title while Vinnie Jones cashed in on his image as a hard man on the football pitch by acting various hard men roles in the movies. As for Madonna, it's doubtful that she would ever have been let near a movie script if she hadn't already been a superstar in the pop world.

2. Be well connected

If you want to get an unfair advantage, probably the best start is to be born into a film family. Most actors who come from this kind of background claim that it makes no difference but imagine what it would be like if your parents were in the movie industry. You'd be on first name terms with directors, actors and technical experts so it would probably be harder not to work in the movie business than to get in on the act.

To avoid people saying that they only got there because of who they know, some actors from famous families even change their name. Nicolas Cage was actually born Nicolas Coppola and is the nephew of famous film director, Francis Coppola.

This director certainly seems happy to keep things in the family as he gave his daughter, Sophia – who was an unknown actress at the time – one of the leading roles in *The Godfather III*. Since then Sophia has paid back the favour. She moved to directing and guess who she employed as assistant director? Her brother.

Other famous film families include the Douglas clan. Kirk Douglas has been in almost 100 films since his first appearance in 1946 and his son Michael Douglas has since followed him in the acting game while his other sons are producers. Any guesses what the latest addition to the family, Dylan Michael Thomas – whose Mum is movie actress Catherine Zeta Jones – might be doing when he gets older?

3. Be exceptional at something

Do you have any unusual hobbies or special skills? Can you whistle the national anthem while riding a micro-scooter and balancing an egg on your nose?

Film scripts often ask for unusual skills and if you've got them, you've got the part.

If you're tough, brave and fearless you may find work as a stunt man or stunt double. Come on, now, you didn't really believe that stars perform all those really dangerous stunts, did you? In fact, most films won't let stars even get their hair out of place as any injury would hold up filming and cost too much money. One major exception was famous Australian star, Mel Gibson, who was actually credited as a stunt man as well as the leading man in the film, *Mad Max 2*. Burt Reynolds, the biggest star of the 70s, also started his career as a stuntman before becoming a leading man.

It's not just special skills that can get you on the silver screen, special characteristics can also come in handy. Instead of spending money on special effects and make-up, Hollywood scouts will scour the planet for people to play unusual roles.

In the first series of Star Wars films, director George Lucas hunted high and low to get actors to fill their roles. Eventually, Peter Mayhew stepped into Chewbacca's furry costume at 2.18 metres while Kenny Baker managed to squeeze all of his 1.12 metre body into R2D2.

One of Hollywood's more ghoulish ways to save money was to cast an actor called Rondo Hatton. After being exposed to poisonous gas in World War Two, this poor man's face was disfigured but the film studios turned this to their advantage and cast him in a series of horror films with the line, 'the monster who needed no make up'. Rondo Hatton was not forgotten and in the 1991 action movie, *The Rocketeer,* the villain's leading henchman was made up to look like him.

The long way round

If you can't take any of these short cuts (and most people can't) the good news is that none of them will stop you becoming a star. The bad news is that it will take you a little bit longer. If there is a traditional route to stardom, then this is it.

Step 1 – go to drama school. Hopefully you'll be able to brush up on your acting and singing skills and get a bit of background on the movie biz. Even more hopefully, you'll make some contacts with people who will go on to open doors for you later on.

Step 2 – get yourself a good publicity photograph and keep it up to date. Most actresses tend to change their photos every three years or so, but male actors are famous for not updating them with the result that their publicity shots often show a young face when the reality is bald and middle-aged.

Step 3 – get yourself an agent. If you're really serious about getting doors opened for you in the movie business, for best results it's well worth going to a professional.

An agent's living depends on the success of the actors they represent. They work hard on your behalf but they don't do it for love – 10% of all your earnings is closer to the mark. So what does an agent do for you? They'll send your show-reels around, make calls, find out when auditions are being held and keep in touch with the latest movies in production. Most reputable casting directors will only agree to audition actors who have been sent to them by trusted agents, so they can be the only way to get your talent spotted.

As you might imagine, getting an agent isn't always easy. They tend to be very busy people but the best way to get one to appreciate your skills is to invite them to watch a play or other production you are in.

FANTASTIC FILM FACT

Agents can be just as eccentric as the actors they represent. One agent was famous for wearing thick black-rimmed glasses when he interviewed hopefuls. However, the glasses were clear and had no lenses in them. If an actor failed to mention them during the meeting, the agent would refuse to represent them.

If you can't find an agent to represent you then don't give up hope. Actors often club together to represent themselves while going it alone is possible but time-consuming. Do you have the confidence to make those calls and can you keep up with what's happening and where? Can you sell yourself to people who need a lot of persuading?

In the end, whether you've got a hot-shot agency backing you up or you're out on your own, all your efforts will be leading in one direction – to getting an audition or a screen-test in front of a director and casting expert.

Awful auditions

At last, it's the moment for you to shine – and the moment most actors dread more than any other. Imagine something more terrifying than a roller-coaster ride, scarier than an encounter with a great white shark or even your physics exams and you'll have an idea how much fun auditions are.

If you're interested in a major part in a film, you'll have an audition that may be followed by a screen test to see how you look on screen. You know that the next few minutes could change your entire life which is why you've been practising your audition piece for weeks. Of course, everyone understands that this could be your first step to superstardom so you're bound to have time to prepare and be given all you need to really shine...

Ow!

That's reality biting for you. Be prepared for the shocking truth about auditions.

If you're an unknown, you'll probably find yourself at an open audition. That means that it's open to anyone, and you can be sure that anyone and everyone will be there. An open audition day probably starts at 6am and begins as you join a long queue snaking around the corner of the building where the auditions are being held. As it starts to rain, you try and forget about the cold, your wet shoes and think about how different it will be when you're famous...

Whether you're famous or not, at a closed or open audition, all actors get nervous because they know that the result is always in doubt. To try and persuade the casting team for *Batman Returns* that she would be perfect for the part, one famous Hollywood star paid for a Catwoman suit to be specially made for her and wore it to the audition. The result? The part went to someone else.

FANTASTIC FILM FACT

Did you know..?

It took almost three years and cost over $100,000 before the longest screen test in history was finally over. After sifting through the 48,768 metres of film that had been shot, producer David O. Selznick finally cast the leading lady for one of the most famous films of all time. It was such a difficult decision that shooting had already begun before he announced that unknown actress, Vivien Leigh, would be the star of the classic 1939 movie *Gone with the Wind.*

It shouldn't happen to an actor

No matter how experienced you are, it's amazing what tricks your nerves can play on you. At audition time, even the most experienced actors can find the simplest tasks beyond them. Some famous stars have had trouble remembering their name, stumbling over their lines or even going to the toilet. We asked some actors to spill the beans on the most awful auditions.

The Short and Long of it

If you're hoping to be cast in a non-speaking role, your audition will probably involve a casting director shouting, "Name... Agent... Look left...Look right... Thank you."

LOOK RIGHT.

LOOK LEFT.

Even if you're going for a speaking part, you may not last much longer. One actor's audition lasted all of two lines before he was told, "You can go now."

When he was still an unknown, Michael Caine didn't even get that far at one audition. He was asked to leave before he had even spoken. The reason was that he was simply too tall for the part. Even if they've got the right skills, the right experience and have done a perfect audition, many actors have been turned down because they're too short, their hair is the wrong colour or their face just doesn't fit the part.

However, some actors have gone through much more to land a part. One ambitious actress went to an audition. It went well and she was called back for a screen test. That passed off successfully so she was invited to do a reading with other cast members. Once again, everything seemed to be going swimmingly and this was confirmed when she went to meet the director. They both got on well and the actress spent the next day excitedly waiting for the call to confirm her part.

Finally the phone rang. She was delighted to hear her agent's voice but was less than delighted when she heard him say, "The director's been replaced and the new person has got their own ideas on who to cast in the part. If you still want the role, you'll have to go through the audition all over again."

Amazingly, she did try but never got past the first stage.

Looking the part

In order to appear in character and help the casting director to make a decision, some actors have turned up at auditions in complete costumes. One hopeful turned up to an audition to play a U-boat captain in boots, jumper and sub-mariner duffel coat even though it was the middle of summer.

Another actor went to the other extreme with his own unusual costume. He had rehearsed a very funny piece and insisted on doing it – in his underpants. It certainly got him noticed and got him the part.

Dos and don'ts

Unfortunately, there are no hard and fast rules for the perfect audition but one actor's experience is a bit like a disaster movie and is so bad that you could use it as a textbook example of exactly what to do and not to do...

Do take it easy beforehand

" *The audition was being held at the end of the day but instead of having plenty of time to prepare, I was travelling down from another production about 160 kilometres away. I planned to arrive in good time but there were serious problems with the trains. As it was, I came out of the tube nearest to the theatre where the auditions were being held with about ten minutes to spare, feeling very hot and bothered.* **"**

Do have time to prepare

" *I was auditioning for the part of a really eccentric character and really wanted to look the part. I thought I wouldn't have the time but as I dashed down the street, I spotted a chemist's and had an idea. I would buy some hair mousse and make my hair stick up at all angles to help me look the part.* **"**

Don't rush when getting ready

"

I was in such a hurry that I bought the mousse and raced into a nearby department store. I spotted a toilet and rushed in to get my hair ready. I squeezed the mousse out of the tube and rubbed it into my hair. It was

only then that I noticed something odd — there was a very strong smell and the hair mousse didn't seem to be rubbing into my hair very well.

To my horror, I took another look at the tube and realised that I had actually bought shaving cream instead of hair mousse ... but the shocks didn't end there. At that moment, the door opened and someone else came into the toilet — a woman. It was only then I noticed that there were only cubicles in the toilets — I was in the Ladies, not the Gents. **"**

Do check you're in the right place

" The only thing to do was run for it. So, with shaving cream dripping from my head and covering my clothes, I picked up my bags, rushed out of the Ladies *and into the theatre... only to be told that I was in the wrong place — the auditions had been moved to a new location across town.* 99

Don't disagree with the director

66 *I felt terrible by the time I arrived — not just because of the sort of day I was having, but also because everyone was still there, waiting for me. Still, I managed to put the nightmares of my day out of my mind and concentrate on my audition. It all went well until the director casually asked me what I thought of the production and I just sort of let it slip that I wasn't a great fan of the script.*

Well, you know those sort of terrible moments when everything goes quiet. It's worse than forgetting your lines and I immediately knew that I wasn't going to be asked to appear in that show. 99

Next?

Of course, it won't mean the end of the world if you do badly – it will only feel like it. Many stars have survived early nightmare outings. The audition notes for musical star, Fred Astaire, read, 'can't act, can't sing, can dance a little' while child star Shirley Temple failed screen tests for several films.

However, if you've given Hollywood your best shot but you think that it just isn't ready to recognise your star qualities, the good news is that your career isn't at the end of the road. You do have some other options for following the yellow brick road to stardom.

If you'd been born about a hundred years ago, you probably wouldn't have had to go far to find a future in films. When moving pictures started to become popular around the world, film studios sprang up in some unlikely locations. Many cities and even some small towns throughout Europe became home to studios.

Unfortunately, the first and second world wars spelt the end for many of these early pioneers as there was little money for equipment and most of their cast were called up to fight or work in factories to help the war effort. The one major country untouched by these wars was America and this led to Hollywood becoming the movie capital of the planet.

However, you may be surprised to hear that Hollywood isn't the only movie city in the world. Bombay is home to the Indian film industry and actually produces more feature films each year than Hollywood. What's more, with millions of fanatical film fans, Bollywood stars are just as popular as their American counterparts.

If India seems too far away, you may have more luck closer to home. Thanks to lottery money, the British movie industry is now growing after decades in decline or you could always cross the channel and star in a French film.

There's one new way to get yourself in front of millions of viewers – the Internet. Movie sites are springing up all the time and some offer you the chance to get involved by voting on a series of plot suggestions and deciding which characters you'd like to stay in or out of the film.

Not having luck with any of these choices? Don't give up. You don't have to be a movie star to make an extremely good living, there's also acting on TV, radio and the theatre that can give you a good career.

6

Tough at the top

However you get there, let's imagine you've finally passed your audition. You've survived the making of your movie and the movie's survived the critics. At last, you've made it, you're now a fully paid-up member of the A-list. But just what can you expect? What will life be like?

First of all, you'd better prepare yourself for a complete and utter change. Normal everyday things like popping down to the shops, jumping on your local bus or even nipping into your local hairdressers are going to go right out of the window. Naturally you'll be amply rewarded for your hard work but you may well be surprised just how much it can cost you in other ways. We give you the low-down on the good side and the flipside of life at the top.

Being in the public eye

Plus points

Being a star certainly has its good bits. For a start, you'll be invited to parties you couldn't get into before, meet lots of new people and you'll also find yourself photographed at the latest movie premieres and in movie magazines.

The flipside

It may be hard to believe but the thrill of going to parties can wear off. And what about all your new friends? Are they interested in you or your money? As for appearing on the news or in magazines, it's great when you've had time to prepare and look like a million dollars but what about those bad hair days when the last thing you want is people taking close-up shots of you?

Having lots of fans

Plus points

Fans are what make your career successful and make you rich. The more popular you become, the bigger your films will become. You'll be able to sell photos of yourself and you'll discover lots of fringe benefits. With all eyes on you, you'll discover people like clothes designers, car manufacturers and perfume makers will be bending over backwards to give you free samples or pay you to advertise their products.

The flipside

It's all very well letting your fans know

about things you want them to know but you'll soon discover that they tend to be interested in every part of your life – even things you'd rather they didn't know about. Perhaps you haven't been entirely honest about your date of birth or your glittering exam results. And what about that disastrous school play you did when you were starting out? You can rest assured that professional reporters will start digging up the dirt on you and your family as they try to find out all about the ups and downs of your life.

Then there's the problem with fans who go a bit too far. Some fans have been known to go through their movie idol's dustbins and while people may

joke that you're not a celebrity until you get a stalker, they're no laughing matter.

Living in a big house

Plus points

With all your money, you'll probably buy a big house for yourself and if you're feeling particularly generous, you may get one for your parents – even your brothers and sisters. You'll be able to furnish it exactly how you like and there's bound to be room for your favourite pinball machine or perhaps a stable for your pony.

The flipside

You may start feeling trapped within the walls, gates, security staff and closed circuit TV that

you need to keep photographers and fans at bay and to protect yourself and your possessions.

Travelling the world

Plus points

As a major star, you'll have great opportunities to visit new and exciting parts of the world. What's more, you can do it in style and travel first class wherever you go.

The flipside

How much of the world will you actually get to see? Everything's fine if you're on holiday but if you're shooting on location, there won't be time for sightseeing. Even worse, if you're on a publicity tour for your latest release you won't see much more than the interior of hotels and airport lounges.

Killer contracts

OK, OK – so life as a star is not all great fun but the truth is that the pros certainly outweigh the cons. If you're big and bossy enough (and you've hired a hot-shot lawyer), you'll find studios happy enough to give you almost anything you want in your contract.

Did you know..?

Jim Carrey caused a bit of double trouble during the filming of the second Ace Ventura film. He had two personal chefs on hand throughout the shoot. One was to prepare meals for him, the other was to prepare meals for his pet iguana.

Looking good doesn't come cheap – but it's not the stars who pay. One big star has her own personal manicurist who charges the studios $75 per nail while another insisted that a make-up assistant was flown from Los Angeles to Malta just to apply some powder to her.

While Julia Roberts was filming one of her movies in New York, a jet plane was kept on standby 24 hours a day in case the star decided she fancied a trip back to Los Angeles.

Of course, this kind of special treatment is only meted out to a few very special stars and only while they remain stars. In fact, it's only now that the real work begins. If you thought it was tough getting to the top, you're in for a surprise.

Once you're at the peak, there's only one way to go – down. If you're determined to stay there, you're going to have a full-time job on your hands fighting off rivals, weeding out bad scripts, avoiding typecasting, the ageing process, bad publicity...

Amazing Animation

Perhaps you're beginning to think that being a star isn't all it's cracked up to be but what options for a life in the movie business does that leave you with? Well, you could consider making your own. Just imagine creating a character that looks just how you want them to look, that wears the clothes you choose for them and does exactly what you want them to do.

It sounds a bit like a scene from a Dr Frankenstein film but in fact, we're talking about animation. Cartoon characters and other animated actors have often turned out to be more popular than their real-life rivals. Think about it for a few seconds and you'll soon realise that for every human star with their name up in lights there's one Mickey Mouse, Buzz Lightyear or Stuart Little hitting the big time.

With 26 Oscars and six special awards under his belt, animation maestro Walt Disney received more Academy Awards than any other person in the movie industry.

At one special ceremony, he was given eight statuettes for his 1937 film, *Snow White and the Seven Dwarfs.* One was full size, the other seven were scaled down versions for each of the dwarfs.

The more you think about it, the more attractive animation becomes. Without a real star, there are no real tantrums, no real contract hassles and no worries about bad behaviour on or off the set. What's more, if you can draw it, model it or create it within a computer, you're well on your way to becoming an animator.

It's all beginning to sound more attractive, isn't it? However, as you are probably beginning to suspect, the animated route to movie success is just as tricky as any other. We give you the low down on how to animate your own career prospects to ensure you're a smash hit rather than a monster flop.

Step 1 – *decide how you're going to animate*

There's a bewildering choice available. If you're good at drawing, you could go down the traditional route and use pen and inks to draw but if you've never mastered anything more complicated than stick people there's still no need to give up hope. Instead, there's computer animation, 3D animation using plasticine or anything else you can lay your creative hands on.

In addition, you might want to try mixing live action with animation and don't forget animatronics either – a technique that combines 3D modelling with puppetry and complex electronics.

Step 2 – *do your research*

If you're stuck on how to breathe life into your creation, take a leaf out of the professionals' book and do your research thoroughly. Animators always pay close attention to the facial expressions and body movements of the characters they're going to animate. Walt Disney was famous for bringing wild animals into his studios for staff to study. Luckily nowadays, with video cameras, you don't need to get quite so close.

Step 3 – *keep an eye on technology*

Animators are only restricted by their imagination and what technology allows them to do. The result is that animators are always pushing back the boundaries to improve their films.

One of the greatest animators and technological geniuses of all time was called Ray Harryhausen. He took stop-motion animation – when an object is moved a tiny amount between each shot – to new heights. He called his new animation system Superdynamation and it worked to great effect in the original *King Kong* movie. Audiences around the world were terrified by this film starring a giant gorilla, but off-screen King Kong was actually a model that was less than 60 cm tall.

Walt Disney studios also came up with some mind-boggling inventions. Their Xeroxing process was used to great effect in *101 Dalmations* but the mother of all technological advances was known as the multiplane camera. Unveiled in 1937, this camera enabled the studio to give depth and dimension to its films, rather than just two dimensional images. The downside of the multiplane camera was that it was nearly six metres tall and required constant attention from two engineering boffins to work out how to use it.

Nowadays, there's more power in your average PC than in Walt Disney's massive camera, and computer programmes are helping animators bring even more advanced and realistic animation to the big screen every year. The arrival of *Toy Story* in 1996 heralded a new stage in animation as it was the first film to have been completely generated on a computer. Even though the stars look real they never actually existed outside their animators' computer screens.

Step 4 – *develop the patience of a saint*

No matter what kind of animation you choose, they all have one thing in common – they take an amazingly long time to get right. Giving your film that seamless, realistic look takes years of practice and most animated films take years in the making.

One scene in the 1963 movie *Jason and the Argonauts* lasted five minutes on screen but took Ray Harryhausen and his crew five months to shoot. Nick Park, the creator of Wallace and Gromit and *Chicken Run*, reckons he's had a good week if five long days shooting produce 30 seconds of film footage.

There's just one last thing to add if you're considering a future in animation.

WARNING:
ANIMATION CAN SERIOUSLY DAMAGE YOUR HEALTH

As it's so slow and complicated, animation can play

tricks on your mind and can turn even the most normal person into a complete animaniac.

This nuttiness was evident in one of the very first animators, a man called Emile Reynaud. After creating a series *Pantomimis Lumineuses* by painting scenes on film strips and showing them through a specially designed projector, he later went a little barmy and threw his invention in the River Seine in Paris.

Trying to act with imaginary cartoon characters can also have strange effects. In films that mix live scenes with animated action, actors often have to act against animated characters that are represented by balloons or balls on sticks before being added into the shot. After six months of being asked to see things on the set of *Who framed Roger Rabbit* in 1988, the film's leading actor started seeing things off it. A course of complete rest was prescribed as the only cure for this case of 'animnesia'.

Behind-the-scenes star

If you decide that animation isn't your cup of tea and you can't act your way out of a paper bag, there's still no need to give up on your dreams of a life in the movie business. The next time you watch a movie, don't head for the exit but stay behind and watch the credits. You may recognise the first two or three names but look at all those other people. For every major star, there are hundreds or even thousands of individuals working in the movie business.

You may not want to take a lead role on camera but you could consider being a star off it. The most powerful behind-the-scenes people are the producers and directors who see their names up in lights as often as their leading actors.

The perils of producing

For real wheeler-dealers, there's only one choice – to consider producing. To do this, you will need to develop a skin that makes a rhinoceros' hide look sensitive along with balancing skills that put a circus acrobat to shame. It can be fabulously well paid but it's also fabulously hard to do.

The first step is to get a script. Once you've got your hands on one, the real producing work begins – raising money for your movie. Perhaps the easiest way to get finance is to cast some big name stars in the movie. If you've got some A-list names, their fans are sure to turn up and once your backers know who's in the frame, they'll stump up the money with few questions asked.

Sounds great, doesn't it? But there's your first problem – how to persuade stars to appear in a film no one's heard of that has no financing behind it? Here's one way of doing it!

Producer: Hey, did you send that script to Bobby?

Assistant: Yup, I biked it over to his house as you said but I don't think it got past the front gate.

Producer: No worries. As long as it got there... now, hand me the phone and I'll call up Stu – he's keen to back a movie. *Phone rings until it is answered.*

Producer: Hey Stu, I've got this great script... Yeah, yeah I know I said it before but this one's dynamite. Bobby's reading it now and he's very excited about it.

Stu: So you're telling me that Bobby's

going to be in it – is that right?

Producer: Yeah, hold on – I've got Steve's agent on the other line... so you like the script? Yeah, and Steve's heard Bobby's going to be in it too... that's right. Yeah, it's getting the green light... what's that? If Bobby's going to be in it, Steve wants in too. Sure, I'll get back to you.

Stu: Did I hear right? You've got Bobby and Steve lined up for the role?

Producer: Sure thing, Stu. So, why don't you drop round the office on Thursday and we'll talk turkey?

So, that's all there is to it?

Well, that's all there is at the start. Then you've got to hold the movie together if one of your stars drops out ... or falls out with the leading lady... or decides they want the script rewritten... or sacks the director... or wants a bigger trailer ... or can't remember their lines... or turns up late...

Demon Directors

If you don't think you're quite cut out for
producing then why not try directing? Throughout
the history of the movies, directors have been
hugely powerful and hugely busy.

Early director, Cecil B. DeMille
was famous for directing
casts of thousands and for
his bossiness. He certainly
dressed the part of a
demon director as he used
to turn up to work in riding
breeches and a riding crop.

Cecil was so busy directing that
he even employed two very specialist assistants to
work for him. These two gofers were paid to follow
him around on set, one to carry his director's chair
and the other to carry his megaphone. It might not
sound too difficult but if they got anything wrong,
the demon director soon lived up to his nickname –
Cecil B. Demented.

While Cecil B. DeMille was certainly busy, he was overshadowed by the work rate of one of the most famous film faces of all time. At the mention of Charlie Chaplin, most people think of the Little Tramp character that he created on screen. However, Charlie didn't just star in all of his movies he also wrote the script, composed the music as well as finding time to direct himself and the rest of the cast.

Not all demon directors were content to stay behind the camera. Famous British director, Alfred Hitchcock was well known for giving himself a small walk-on role in almost all of his films. If you're a movie fan, you can play 'spot the director' on the silver screen.

You've probably heard of Steven Spielberg, George Lucas and perhaps some other big name directors like Orson Welles but what about Alan (or Allen) Smithee? This director first appeared in 1969 on the credits for *Death of a Gunfighter* and has appeared regularly ever since. So what's so unusual about him? The answer is that he doesn't actually exist.

It may sound like the plot for a movie thriller but the explanation is simple. The name Alan Smithee is used in the credits if a studio takes control of a film from the director and makes changes to it against his or her wishes. In past Alan Smithee films, the original director's cut has been shortened drastically, made longer and one even had an entirely new ending added on.

So, if you spot the name 'Alan Smithee' on the credits, be warned. It doesn't necessarily mean that it's going to be a bad movie, but it means that you'll not be watching the film that the original director wanted you to see.

Name that job

Directing and producing aren't the only opportunities available. Check out the credits and you'll see plenty of other jobs but some of them have some very strange names indeed. Before you consider applying, we'll put you in the picture about what they mean. Why not see if you can pass our behind-the-scenes screen test by matching the job title to its description?

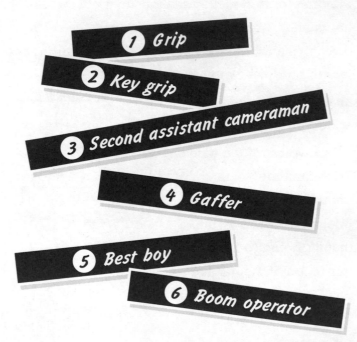

1 Grip

2 Key grip

3 Second assistant cameraman

4 Gaffer

5 Best boy

6 Boom operator

A Chief electrician on set. Responsible for ensuring a smooth and safe flow of power to the camera, lights, sound and special effects crews.

B Removal person. Your job is to move any equipment around the set.

C Strong arms required. You'll be operating the microphone on set ensuring it's close enough to pick up the actors' speeches but that it doesn't appear in shot.

D As well as loading films for the cinematographer, you'll also have one of the most famous jobs around — operating the clapperboard at the start of each new take.

E This important role involves moving that vital piece of equipment, the camera, around the set.

F You'll be assisting the electrician on set — and you can be female to do the job.

Answers: 1B, 2E, 3D, 4A, 5F, 6C.

Fab five movie jobs

Haven't yet found something that's right up your street? There are still plenty of jobs available and we give you the inside track on our favourite five movie occupations. Which one would suit you best?

Location scout

Job description: to track down the right locations for movies.

Special skills: must be highly mobile and like a true boy scout, be prepared to drop everything to track down suitable film locations.

Special equipment:
Always carry a world atlas. If you're filming an outer space epic like *Star Wars*, quarries or the Sahara desert are always good stand-bys.

Trade secrets: be imaginative.

The futuristic city of Metropolis in *Superman IV* was actually shot in Milton Keynes while the Yorkshire Moors were re-created in California for *Wuthering Heights*.

If you can't find the right house for a shoot, choose two. In the *Batman* movie, two houses were used for Wayne Manor. The interior shots are of Hatfield House while the exterior shows Knebworth House.

Continuity editor

Job description: to ensure that visual details don't change between takes and to keep a sharp eye out for anything that may have changed.

Special skills: a keen eye for detail and plenty of patience to ensure that everything looks the same, even though it might be days between takes.

Special equipment: carry a large bag or a case to store shots of the final frames at the end of cut.

Trade secrets: develop a thick skin and don't rely on your memory.

If you do your job well, no one will notice. It's only when mistakes have been made that audiences notice.

Wardrobe assistant

Job description: to find costumes for an entire cast, alter them as necessary and ensure they survive throughout the film.

Special skills: good research skills are necessary to find the correct clothes and good sewing skills are also necessary.

Trade secrets: be flexible, you never know what you'll be asked to do in your job.

Always remember that not all costumes need to be good as new. Shoe polish and dirt are often rubbed into costumes to give them that authentic battered look. One wardrobe assistant working on a film in South America was given the order to swap the brand new ponchos she had been given for battered garments belonging to local people.

By contrast, space age technology was incorporated in Captain Hook's costume in the movie *Hook*. The captain's pirate gear was so hot and heavy that the actor inside had to wear an air-conditioned jacket that had originally been developed for astronauts.

Make-up artiste

Job description: to develop make-up that will make stars look good or to create unique looks for actors that will withstand the hot lights and any other special effects thrown at them.

Special skills: calm hands and seriously good make-up skills will be needed as you stroke and caress those sensitive artists. You'll also need to be discreet as you're getting a closer look at some famous faces who might not be happy if you reveal any spots or wrinkles that may have appeared.

Special equipment: always carry a large box of special stage make-up.

Trade secret: be prepared to improvise.

We let you in on some ingenious make-up methods.

Cereal killer – if you're making up someone to be a witch, you'll need some rice crispies. Add some milk to soften them and mould them to your actor's face to create a horrible wart. Pop a false hair into the centre for added revoltingness.

A cut above – need to give someone an oozing cut or a bubbling boil? Solve the problem by mixing flour and water and add to the skin. Add red or yellow food colours for that final revolting touch.

Animal trainer

Job description: you'll need to be able to get on with animals. You'll be responsible for getting them to and from the sets and for looking after them between takes. You'll also be in charge of them when they're in front of the camera to ensure they do as they are supposed to.

Special skills: from dogs to ducks, iguanas to tarantulas, you'll have to get on with the widest variety of animals that a director could ever want.

Special equipment: a large supply of the right food. Most animals are harmless when they are full so always carry plentiful supplies of the

appropriate food to
ensure they get their
teeth into their role – not
any part of your body.

Trade secrets: never
show an animal you're
afraid. Whatever the
species, you should
always be in control.

Be prepared. Whatever the job, you should always
have the right equipment for handling your
animals.

Closing scene

So there you have it. Now you've got the low-down on some of the jobs available behind the silver screen and when it comes to climbing the slippery steps to stardom, we've well and truly let the cat out of the bag.

As you've probably gathered, despite the magic of the movies, all jobs in the film industry have one thing in common – they are incredibly hard work. So, why are so many people keen to make sacrifices, to push themselves harder than they thought possible and to work long hours?

Perhaps Alfred Hitchcock, the famous director

had the answer when he described film as 'life with all the boring bits taken out'. One thing you can be sure of is that life in the movie industry is never dull. Whatever your job title is, you can never be sure what you'll be doing next. If you're a star, one day you might be filming a historical drama one minute then acting in a sci-fi thriller the next. As a stunt double, you could be throwing yourself out of a helicopter or driving through explosions. In the costume business, you might be juggling a project to research medieval armour along with tracking down the right kind of suit for a 20s gangster movie.

If you've got the grit, determination and talent, there's no reason why you can't succeed for yourself in the movie industry. And even if you don't, at the very least, you can still enjoy watching all that hard work look so easy at your local cinema.